D1546825

God Made
Girls & Boys

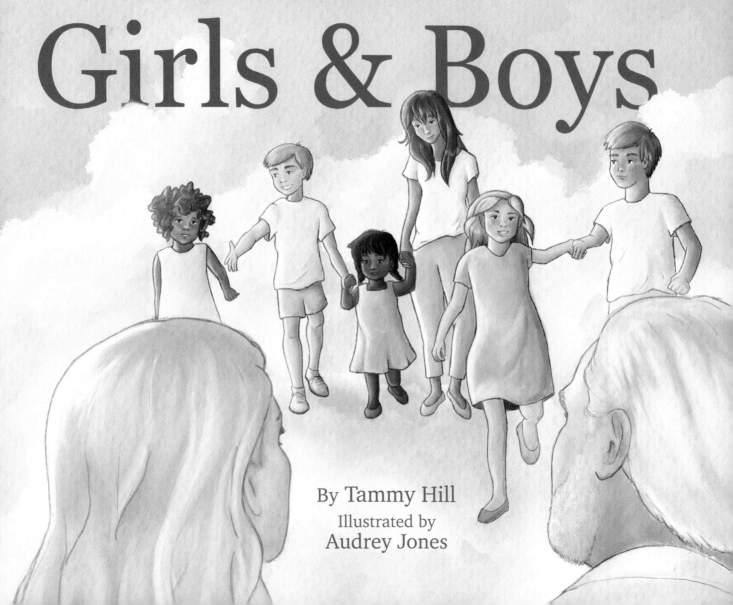

By Tammy Hill

Illustrated by
Audrey Jones

You lived in heaven before you were born.

Before we came to earth, we lived as spirits
in heaven. Some spirits were boys and
some spirits were girls. We lived together
as brothers and sisters in one big family. In
heaven, we have a Father and a Mother, who
love us. They are the Parents of our spirits.

You are a child of Heavenly Parents.

Heavenly Father and Heavenly Mother were different from Their spirit children. They had physical bodies! Their spirits lived inside of Their bodies. Their spirits and Their bodies worked in harmony. When a body jumps, the spirit inside that body also jumps. When a body smiles, the spirit also smiles. Our Heavenly Father and Heavenly Mother are equally important but physically different from each other.

How do you think Heavenly Father and Heavenly Mother are alike? How are They different?

You wanted a body.

We, the spirit children of our Heavenly Parents, wanted physical bodies too. We wanted to be able to do what we saw Them do. With bodies we would be able to experience everything more fully. We could smell flowers, taste oranges, and feel warm hugs from our parents.

They told us about a plan that would make it possible for us to have bodies too. Male spirits could have a body that looks and works like Heavenly Father's. Female spirits could have a body that looks and works like Heavenly Mother's. We were excited to become more like Them.

Why do you think you wanted a body?

You can choose to feel happy.

Our Heavenly Parents called Their plan "the plan of happiness." They know that by choosing to follow this plan we can be happy like They are. We understood that we could choose between right and wrong. We chose what to do in heaven. We choose what to do on earth. This is agency. The plan also includes accountability. This means that we are responsible for the choices we make. For example, if you do something wrong, like take something that belongs to someone else, you feel bad and worry you will get in trouble. Or, if you do something good like draw a picture and leave it on your mom's pillow, you feel happy.

What are some choices you have made? How have these choices made you feel?

You can pray for help to make good choices.

We needed to leave heaven so that we could learn and grow with our bodies. We don't remember our time in heaven while we are on earth. But we can pray to our Heavenly Father and learn about His Son, Jesus Christ. Doing these things helps us remember that we are children of a loving Heavenly Father and Heavenly Mother, who want us to learn to make choices that allow us to be happy like They are.

Why do you think we cannot remember our time in Heaven?

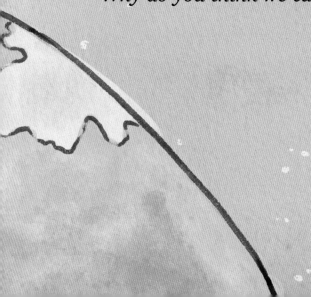

Adam and Eve came to earth first.

Adam and Eve were the first man and woman to get bodies.
Together, as husband and wife, they started the first family on earth.
And just like our Heavenly Parents, Adam and Eve were created to
be equally important but physically different from each other.

How are Adam and Eve alike? How are they different from each other?

Together a man and a woman can make a baby.

A very important part of the plan of happiness allows us to create families, just like Adam and Eve. When a man and woman get married, a new family is made. Together a husband and wife can become a father and mother by creating a baby. Heavenly Father and Heavenly Mother want fathers and mothers on earth to work together to love, protect, and teach their children.

How do you know that your father and mother love you?

You started your time on earth as a baby.

When you were born your spirit and body came together. One of the first things parents say when a baby is born is "It's a boy!" or "It's a girl!" A baby girl will grow up to have a body that works and looks like her mother's body. A baby boy will grow up to have a body that works and looks like his father's body.

What do your parents remember about the day you were born? What did your parents say when they first saw you?

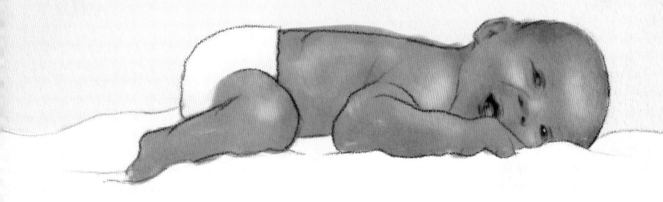

Your spirit has a body!

You can do so many wonderful things with your body! You can see sunsets, hear birds chirp, taste watermelon, and smell roses. You can touch things that are hot or cold, prickly or smooth. You learn what it feels like to be hungry or tired. You learn that some things feel really wonderful, like warm, safe hugs or soft, fluffy pillows. Your spirit is learning so much by being inside of your body!

What are some things your spirit has learned inside of your body?

Your body and spirit work together.

When your body jumps, your spirit jumps. When your body smiles, your spirit smiles. To keep your body and spirit healthy you need to drink water, eat good food, and get enough sleep. You need to work, play in the sunshine, and breathe deeply to help your body and spirit feel connected. You need to learn to read and write, make things with your hands, and use your imagination to help your body and spirit express what makes you special.

What do you love to do? What is something you do that helps you feel special?

Your family loves you.

You need relationships with other people, like your parents, family, and friends. These people can help you feel important and connected. Some day, you may choose to be married. When a husband and wife share their love in a marriage relationship, it is one of the ways they can feel very happy and complete.

Who loves you? Who do you love?

Your body can do so many things.

It is amazing how your Heavenly Mother and Heavenly Father, along with your earthly mother and earthly father, made you. There is no one on earth who is just like you! Girls and boys are equally important but physically different. Both girls and boys can develop their bodies through many activities, such as sports, dance, music, and art.

What are some of your favorite activities? Why?

On earth you can feel peace when you remember why you are here.

Long before you came to earth, our Heavenly Father and Heavenly Mother planned a way for you to be born. You chose to follow Their plan in heaven. They want you to remember Their plan as your body and spirit work together on earth. As you study and pray to know what to do, you can feel the difference between right and wrong. Remember that you are part of a heavenly family. You are a son or daughter of Heavenly Parents. Remember who you are.

What choices have you made that help you feel peaceful and happy? What do you understand better by reading this book?

For Mark—the man in my dreams

For Jeff—the man who makes all my dreams come true

I love you both.

Copyright © 2021 Tammy Hill.

All rights reserved. No part of this work covered by the copyright herein may be reproduced or used in any form or by any means–graphic, electronic, or mechanical, including photocopying, recording, taping, web distribution or information storage and retrieval systems without the written permission of the copyright holders.

ISBNs:
9781736296707 (Paperback)
9781736296714 (Hardback)

Printed in South Korea